Pictorial Guide to National Orchid Garden

国家胡姬园指南
国立蘭園ガイドブック

Contents

Sponsor	6
Introduction	8
Use of Guide	12
"spring" zone	18-25
"summer" zone	26-30
"autumn" zone	31-44
"winter" zone	45-51
Orchidarium	52-61
VIP Orchid Garden	62
Burkill Hall	65
Index of orchids	67
Acknowledgements	68

内容

前言	9
游览指引图的使用	13
"春"分区	18-25
"夏"分区	26-30
"秋"分区	31-44
"冬"分区	45-51
胡姬原种区	52-61
贵宾胡姬园	63
伯克厅	65
胡姬索引	67

目次

前書き	10
当ガイドのみかた	14
「春」ゾーン	18-25
「夏」ゾーン	26-30
「秋」ゾーン	31-44
「冬」ゾーン	45-51
オーキダリウム（ラン栽培園）	52-61
VIP ラン園	63
バーキル ホール	66
ランの目録	67

Sponsor

Singapore Botanic Gardens, the National Parks Board, acknowledges the generous sponsorship of Singapore Airlines, for the publication of this guide.

A new hybrid, **Dendrobium Singapore Girl Orchid**, was named on 12 June 1997 to commemorate the 50th anniversary of Singapore Airlines Limited.

"新加坡女郎"石斛兰

"新加坡女郎"石斛兰取名于1997年6月12日,为新加坡航空公司成立50周年志庆。

国家胡姬园游览指引图蒙新加坡航空公司赞助出版,国家公园局特此鸣谢。

デンドロビウム シンガポール ガール

デンドロビウム シンガポール ガールというランの花名は1997年6月12日に、シンガポール航空の50周年記念にちなんで、命名されました。

この「国立ラン園写真案内」の作成にあたり、シンガポール航空株式会社によるご支援に感謝の意を表します。

Dendrobium Singapore Girl Orchid

Introduction

The National Orchid Garden is located on the highest hill in the Singapore Botanic Gardens. Three hectares of its gentle eastern slopes were carefully landscaped to provide a setting for 60,000 orchid plants comprising 400 species and more than 2,000 hybrids.

The design concept of the National Orchid Garden presents plants in four separate colour zones achieved by a careful blend of orchids (mostly hybrids) and other ornamentals selected for their matching hues of foliage and flowers.

The terraced slopes and pathways were designed to be accessible by the handicapped. Fountains and waterfalls were sculptured and strategically located to complement the plants displayed and to provide a sparkling fresh effect in a lush tropical Garden.

Upon entering through the Ticketing Pavilion, visitors are greeted by a cascading fountain featuring a pair of bronze cranes. This is the "spring" zone of the Garden where prevailing colours are bright and lively shades of gold, yellow and cream.

Adjacent is the vibrant "summer" zone where the major tones are the various shades of strong red and pink. Then the matured "autumn" shades beckon, and finally the "winter" garden of white and cool blue.

Special features include the VIP (Very Important Plant) display. VIPs are outstanding hybrids from the Singapore Botanic Gardens named after state visitors and other dignitaries ... *Vandaenopsis* **Nelson Mandela**, *Dendrobium* **Memoria Princess Diana**, *Renantanda* **Prince Norodom Sihanouk**, *Dendrobium* **Margaret Thatcher**, *Renantanda* **Akihito** ... to name a few.

In a leafy section is the Orchidarium where the species collection is nurtured. Further along the meandering path are two misthouses which allow for special displays in a more intimate and conducive environment.

The Tan Hoon Siang misthouse features orchids displayed against a backdrop of cultural decor and the Yuen-Peng McNeice bromeliad collection presents a display of over 20,000 plants representing over 800 types in the Pineapple family.

Rounding off a visit to the National Orchid Garden make a stop at **Burkill Hall** at the top of the hill. Completed in 1866, this British colonial home of former directors of the Singapore Botanic Gardens has been carefully restored to serve as a reception centre.

前言

国家胡姬园坐落于新加坡植物园内最高的山坡。其占地三公顷的东向斜坡经精心设计,展示六万株胡姬,包括了四百个原种和超过两千个配种。

国家胡姬园的设计概念,是通过对多种胡姬(主要是配种)和根据叶片与花朵色泽选用的观赏植物的细心安排,揉合成四个颜色分区的花卉展示场。

沿山坡而筑的石阶与小径,设计时考虑到残障人士行走的方便。喷泉与瀑布全加上雕刻装饰,并讲究安置的地点,藉此为青翠热带园林增添几许亮丽和清新。

游客经过售票亭进入园中,即刻受到喷泉上方两只黄铜铸造的仙鹤的恭迎。这是"春"分区,主色是明亮、充满生气的金、黄及乳白。

毗邻是具震撼性的"夏"分区,主要的色调是强烈的艳红与粉红。接着迎来成熟的"秋"色,最后是白与蓝色的"冬"园。

国家胡姬园的特色包括贵宾兰花的展示。所谓贵宾兰花指的是新加坡植物园以国宾及其他达官显贵命名的特出胡姬配种,如尼森曼德拉蝴蝶梵兰、纪念戴安娜王妃石斛兰、西哈诺亲王肾梵兰、玛格烈撒切尔石斛兰、明仁太子肾梵兰等。

叶片繁茂的胡姬原种区,是培植来自世界各地胡姬原种的地方。沿着蜿蜒的小径走去,旁边有两间雾室,充作展示需要特别生长环境的品种的用途。

陈温祥雾室以各国文化装饰为背景展示各国胡姬配种,麦婉平夫人凤梨科温室则展示了八百多种凤梨科植物共两万株。

国家胡姬园的游人最后可在山坡顶端的伯克厅停下歇脚,圆满结束整个行程。伯克厅建于1866年,英殖民地时曾是新加坡植物园几任前总管的住宅。经过全面翻新,现在是国家胡姬园的接待中心。

前書き

国立ラン園は、植物園で一番高い丘の東側斜面を取り巻くように造られています。3ヘクタールの広さのなだらかな斜面に、現在、四百種、二千もの交配品種からなる六万本を越えるランが美しい花々を咲かせています。

当ラン園のデザイン・コンセプトは4つの独立したカラーゾーンから成ります。各ゾーンには、様々なラン（その大半は交配品種）が効果的に配置されており、葉や花の色彩にあわせた庭園装飾で四季が演出されています。

高台へは、当園に備え付けの車椅子でも簡単に上れるように、ゆるやかな道がつけられています。丘の上の成長した木々は、当園を訪れる人々に憩いの木陰をつくり噴水や滝は涼をよんでくれます。

切符売り場を通って入園すると、つがいの鶴のブロンズ像が立つ「鶴の噴水」に迎えられます。そこは、もうラン園の「春」ゾーン。金色、黄色、クリーム色の陰影を配した、明るい色調で春のイメージが表現されています。

「春」ゾーンから、活気あふれる赤と明るいピンクで織り成される「夏」ゾーンに続き、おちついた色使いの「秋」ゾーンへと移って行きます。そして最後に、白と冷たい青色の庭園、「冬」ゾーンへと続いて行きます。

当ラン園独特の特徴のひとつに、VIPランの展示があります。VIPランには、国賓や、シンガポール国内、国外のVIPに敬意を表して、当植物園からの選りすぐった混成種に、その名を組み合わせた花名がつけられています。バンダ　ノプシス　ネルソン　マンデラ、デンドロビウム　メモリア　プリンセス　ダイアナ、レナンタンダ　プリンス　ノロドム　シアヌーク、デンドロビウム　マーガレット　サッチャー、レナンタンダ　アキヒト、などが挙げられます。

オーキダリウム（ラン栽培園）は、当植物園のコレクションと交配種が栽培されている、緑の鮮やかなスペースです。そこから進む曲がりくねった小道は、ミストハウスの入り口へと続きます。ミストハウスでは、ランがより良く観賞できるよう、ディスプレイに特別な趣向が凝らされています。

タン　フーン　シアン　ミストハウスには古代文明調の庭園装飾の中に、めずらしいランの数々が展示されていま

す。また、ユエン ペン マクニース ブロメリアド コレクションでは、パイナップル科の八百種類、二万本もの観葉植物やエアープラント等を見ることができます。

さらに、丘の頂上まで歩いていくと、19世紀に建てられたイギリス植民地時代のクラシックな住宅、バーキル ホールが迎えてくれます。この建て物は、1866年に完成しシンガポール植物園の歴代の園長の住まいとして使われて来ましたが、現在、元通りに修復され、レセプション センターとして利用されています。

Use of Guide to National Orchid Garden:

For the convenience of visitors, the orchids and features of the National Orchid Garden are marked on the map by numbers.

"spring" zone
1. Crane Fountain
2. *Oncidium* Goldiana 'Golden Shower'
3. *Mokara* Kelvin 'Yellow'
4. *Dendrobium* Chanel
5. Tiger Orchid Fountain
6. *Arachnis* Maggie Oei
7. *Mokara* Zaleha Alsagoff
8. *Mokara* Sayan

"summer" zone
9. *Mokara* Chark Kuan
10. *Aranthera* Beatrice Ng 'Yellow'
11. *Ascocenda* Peggy Foo
12. *Renantanda* Charlie Mason
13. Waterfall

"autumn" zone
14. *Vanda* Miss Joaquim
15. *Vanda* Miss Joaquim 'Douglas'
16. *Sophrolaeliocattleya* Hawaiian Starlet
17. *Mokara* Bibi
18. *Vanda* Ruby Prince
19. *Aranda* Majula 'Rimau'
20. *Mokara* Kelvin 'Orange'
21. *Stamariaara* Noel
22. *Christieara* Malibu Gold
23. *Vanda* Margaret Tan
24. *Dendrobium* hybrids
24a. *Dendrobium* Seena
24b. *Dendrobium* White Fairy
24c. *Dendrobium* Genting Blue
24d. *Dendrobium* Hiang Beauty
25. *Lewisara* Fatimah Alsagoff

"winter" zone
26. *Vanda* Poepoe 'Diana'
27. *Aranda* Wong Bee Yeok
28. *Dendrobium crumenatum*
29. *Aranda* Christine 'Alba'
30. Tan Hoon Siang misthouse
31. Yuen-Peng McNeice bromeliad house
32. Sundials
33. Orchidarium
33a. *Dendrobium bigibbum* 'compactum'
33b. Terrestrial orchids
33c. Lithophytic orchids
33d. Epiphytic orchids
33e. Slipper orchids
33f. Orchidarium waterfall
33g. *Arundina graminifolia*
33h. Rat Tail Orchid
33i. *Epidendrum cinnabarinum*
34. VIP Orchid Garden
35. Burkill Hall

国家胡姬园游览指引图

国家胡姬园游览指引图的使用：

为了游人的方便，国家胡姬园把园内的胡姬与景点，根据其所在分区的位置，以编号标示在地图上。

"春"分区

1. 仙鹤喷泉
2. 金黄瘤唇兰变种金阵雨
3. 卡明黄莫氏兰
4. 婵娜石斛兰
5. 虎兰喷泉
6. 马奇威蜻蜓兰
7. 沙里哈阿沙戈夫莫氏兰
8. 沙扬莫氏兰

"夏"分区

9. 扎宽莫氏兰
10. 贝特立诗黄蜓肾兰
11. 柏琪符壶唇梵兰
12. 查理马松肾梵兰
13. 瀑布

"秋"分区

14. 卓锦万代兰
15. 卓锦万代兰变种"道格拉斯"
16. 夏威夷坦乐朱色蕾利卡德丽亚兰
17. 比比莫氏兰
18. 鲁比太子万代兰
19. 马珠拉"里茂"蜻蜓万代兰
20. 卡明橙色莫氏兰
21. 惹尔史打马利亚氏兰
22. 马里布金黄克里斯蒂氏兰
23. 马格烈陈万代兰
24. 石斛兰杂交品种
24a. 西娜石斛兰
24b. 白仙女石斛兰
24c. 云顶蓝石斛兰
24d. 香尔美女石斛兰
25. 法地马阿沙戈夫卢娃沙拉兰

"冬"分区

26. 泊泊"蒂娜"万代兰
27. 黄美玉蜻蜓万代兰
28. 鸠斛兰
29. 克丽斯汀"亚巴"蜻蜓万代兰
30. 陈温祥雾室
31. 麦婉平夫人风梨科温室
32. 日晷仪
33. 胡姬原种区
33a. 碧姬蔓石斛兰
33b. 地生类胡姬
33c. 岩石生类胡姬
33d. 附生类胡姬
33e. 拖鞋兰
33f. 胡姬原种区瀑布
33g. 穗叶竹兰
33h. 鼠尾兰
33i. 树兰
34. 贵宾胡姬园
35. 伯克厅

国立ラン園のガイドのみかた：

訪問者の便宜のために、国立ラン園では、地図に番号を記入して、それぞれの位置がよくわかるように提示しています。

「春」ゾーン

1. 鶴の噴水
2. オンシヂウム　ゴルディアナ　"ゴールデン　シャワー"
3. モカラ　ケルビン　"イエロー"
4. デンドロビウム　シャネル
5. タイガー　オーキッドの噴水
6. アラクニス　マギー　オーイ
7. モカラ　ザレハ　アルサゴフ
8. モカラ　サヤン

「夏」ゾーン

9. モカラ　チャーク　クアン
10. アランセラ　ベヤトリス　ン　"イエロー"
11. アスコセンダ　ペギー　フー
12. レナンタンダ　・　チャーリー　メイソン
13. 滝

「秋」ゾーン

14. バンダ　ミス　ジョーキム
15. バンダ　ミス　ジョーキム　"ダグラス"
16. ソフィロラエリオカトレア　ハワイアン　スターレット

17. モカラ　ビビ
18. バンダ　ルビー　プリンス
19. アランダ　マジュラ　"リマウ"
20. モカラ　ケルビン　"オレンジ"
21. スタマリアーラ　ノエル
22. クリスチアーラ　マリブー　ゴールド
23. バンダ　マーガレット　タン
24. デンドロビウム　交配種
24a. デンドロビウム　シーナ
24b. デンドロビウム　ホワイト　フェアリー
24c. デンドロビウム　ゲンティン　ブルー
24d. デンドロビウム　ヒアン　ビューティー
25. ルーイサラ　ファティマ　アルサゴフ

「冬」ゾーン

26. バンダ　ポーポー　"ダイアナ"
27. アランダ　ウオン　ビー　イョク
28. デンドロビウム　クルメナタム
29. アランダ　クリスチーン　"アルバ"
30. タン　フーン　シアン　ミストハウス
31. ユエン　ペン　マクニース　ブロメリアド　ハウス
32. 日時計
33. オーキダリウム（ラン栽培園）
33a. デンドロビウム　ビギバン

33b. 陸生ラン
33c. 岩石生ラン
33d. 上部着生ラン
33e. スリッパーラン
33f. 滝
33g. アランディナ　グラミニフォリア
33h. ねずみのしっぽラン
33i. エピデンドラム　シンナバリナム

34. VIPラン園

35. バーキル　ホール

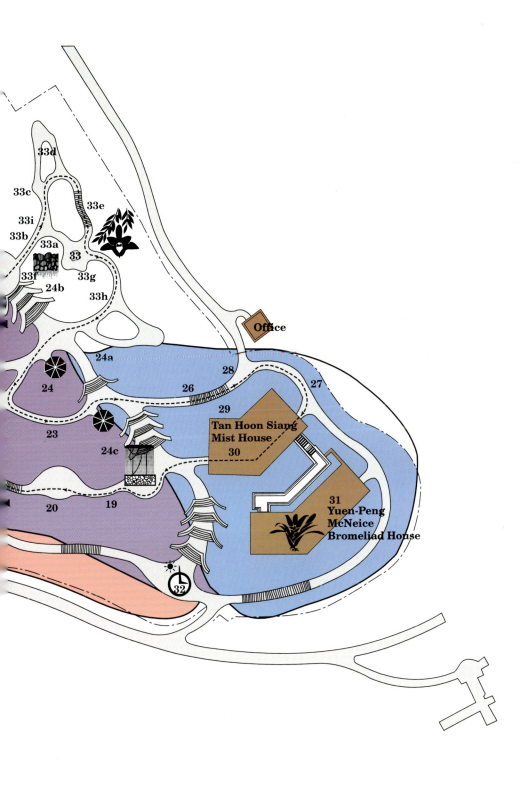

1. Crane Fountain

The Crane Fountain located just beyond the Entrance Pavilion is a popular photographic spot. Two bronze cranes, perched on the top of the fountain, greet you as you enter the Gardens. The cranes symbolise good health and longevity.

Crane Fountain

1. 仙鹤喷泉

仙鹤喷泉座落于进口处亭子的后面,是游人拍照留念的热门景点。青铜铸成的两只仙鹤,栖息在喷泉顶端,恭迎客人的光临。仙鹤象征健康长寿。

1. 鶴の噴水

入口の建て物を越えてすぐに位置する鶴の噴水は、人気の写真撮影スポットとなっています。つがいの鶴のブロンズ像は、あたかも入園者たちを歓迎するかのように、噴水の上に止まっています。鶴は健康と長寿の象徴でもあります。

2. *Oncidium* Goldiana
   'Golden Shower'
   This is an early hybrid from the Singapore Botanic Gardens. It has earned the name "Dancing Lady" because of the beautiful and elegant yellow flowers. The overall impression is that of a ball-room dancer in a voluminous skirt.

2. 金黄瘤唇兰变种金阵雨
   金黄瘤唇兰变种金阵雨是新加坡植物园早期培育出来的配种。金阵雨花以标致及优雅的黄色花朵，赢得了"起舞的淑女"的美誉。就总体印象来说，金阵雨花犹如穿着宽裙在舞池中翩翩起舞的女郎。

Oncidium Goldiana 'Golden Shower'

2. オンシヂウム　ゴルディアナ"ゴールデン　シャワー"
   このランはシンガポール植物園の初期の交配品種です。美しい黄色の花はそのエレガントな姿ゆえに、"ダンシング　レディー"とも呼ばれ、舞踏会の踊り子の優雅なドレスを思わせます。

Mokara Kelvin 'Yellow'

3. ***Mokara* Kelvin 'Yellow'**
This is an early ***Mokara*** produced in Singapore. The plant is very free flowering. This hybrid is grown in full sun which encourages flowering. The small dainty flowers are popular in the cut-flower trade and after 20 years, still in popular demand.

3. **卡明黄莫氏兰**
卡明黄莫氏兰是新加坡较早期生产的莫氏兰品种。这是长年开花的品种。在艳阳下生长，烈日下花朵盛开。花朵娇小雅致，在剪花枝市场很受欢迎。即使二十年后，需求依旧强劲。

3. **モカラ　ケルビン　"イエロー"**
シンガポールでつくられた初期のモカラで、大変簡単に花を咲かせることができます。この交配品種は、開花を促す充分な太陽光のもとで育成されます。花は小さく、優美で、切り花として多く売られ、二十年を経たいまも市場の人気者です。

4. ***Dendrobium* Chanel**

This Singapore hybrid with pastel coloured flowers is very popular with our Japanese visitors. This vigorous hybrid is easy to grow. It blooms all year round and produces very lasting flowers making it very popular as a cut-flower.

4. 婵娜石斛兰

新加坡培育的婵娜石斛兰，花朵呈清淡的粉紫色，深受日本游客喜爱。此配种生命力强，长年开花，花期持久，在剪花枝市场极受欢迎。

Dendrobium Chanel

4. **デンドロビウム　シャネル**

パステル調のやわらかい色味をもつこのランは、シンガポールでの交配品種のひとつで、日本人の訪問客のあいだで絶大な人気を得ています。繁殖力旺盛で、手間がかかりません。一年を通じて花をつけ、花もちがよく、切り花として絶大な人気があります。

5. Tiger Orchid Fountain

Growing on top of this fountain is the Tiger Orchid, ***Grammatophyllum speciosum***, so named because markings on the flowers resemble patterns on the skin of the tiger.

The largest of orchids, a good specimen can weigh over one ton. A flowering spray can reach 2m in length and a plant may bear thousands of flowers.

5. 虎兰喷泉

盘踞在这喷泉顶端的虎兰，也称为巨兰，因为花瓣上的斑纹就像虎皮一样，所以得名。

虎兰是世界最大的胡姬品种，一棵成长的虎兰重量可达一吨以上。其花枝可长达两米，一株可生多达千朵花。

5. タイガー オーキッドの噴水

噴水のてっぺんに植えられているのがタイガー オーキッドで、別名グラマトフィラム スペシオサムといい、花びらの模様が虎に似ているところからこう呼ばれています。世界最大のランでもあり、成長した木は、1トン以上もの重さになり、無数の花がつく小枝は2メートルにも及びます。

Tiger Orchid Fountain

6. *Arachnis* Maggie Oei

This hybrid is commonly known as the Scorpion Orchid. It is extremely vigorous and free-flowering and is ideal as a cut-flower. It was one of the earliest cut-flowers to be exported from Singapore, being popular in the 1950s and 60s.

6. 马奇威蜻蜓兰

马奇威蜻蜓兰花型像蝎子，俗称蝎兰。此花生命力极强，长年开花，是理想的剪花枝品种。马奇威蜻蜓兰是新加坡最早的剪花枝出口品种之一，五六十年代极为风行。

6. アラクニス マギー オーイ

通称、スコーピオン オーキッド。この交配品種は、繁殖力旺盛で、花も咲かせやすいので、切り花として広く親しまれています。1950～60年代に人気のあった、シンガポールから輸出された初期の切り花のひとつでもありました。

Arachnis Maggie Oei

7. *Mokara* Zaleha Alsagoff

This award winning orchid is one of the larger-sized yellow ***Mokara*** hybrids. The plant is easy to grow and is free flowering once it is well established.

7. 沙里哈阿沙戈夫莫氏兰

沙里哈阿沙戈夫莫氏兰是得奖的品种，属于较大型的黄色莫氏兰配种。容易栽种，一旦成长，就能长年开花。

7. モカラ ザレハ アルサゴフ

賞を獲得したことのあるこのランは、大きな黄金のモカラの一種です。いったんうまく栽培すれば、どんどん育ち開花させやすい品種です。

Mokara Zaleha Alsagoff

8. ***Mokara* Sayan**
   A popular potted orchid as the plant is small and compact. This hybrid is outstanding as the flowers do not bear spots common in most ***Mokara*** hybrids. This free-flowering hybrid is also popular as a cut-flower.

8. **沙扬莫氏兰**
   沙扬莫氏兰因为体型娇小，花朵稠密，是一种深受欢迎的盆栽胡姬。这一配种特出的地方是其花瓣不带斑点，有别于一般带斑点的莫氏兰。长年开花的沙扬莫氏兰也是深受欢迎的剪花枝胡姬。

8. **モカラ サヤン**
   小さくコンパクトなので、鉢植えとして人気があり、また、大半のモカラ種の中でも花びらに班点がない点できわ立っています。花も咲かせやすく、切り花としても人気があります。

Mokara Sayan

Mokara Chark Kuan

9. ***Mokara* Chark Kuan**
An interesting plant bred in Malaysia. It is popular in the cut-flower trade. There are several differently coloured varieties of this free flowering hybrid.

9. **扎宽莫氏兰**
扎宽莫氏兰是马来西亚培育出来的有趣品种，在剪花枝市场极受欢迎。长年开花的扎宽莫氏兰会开出多种不同颜色的花朵。

9. **モカラ　チャーク　クアン**
この人の目を惹きつけるランは、マレーシアで多く見られる品種です。切り花として人気がありますが、花はもともと単色で、品種改良の結果、現在のように複数の色をもつようになりました。

10. *Aranthera* Beatrice Ng 'Yellow'

This hybrid won an award at the World Orchid Conference in 1964. The flowering sprays are long and branching, bearing more than 60 yellow flowers each. After more than 30 years, this hybrid is still popular as a cut-flower.

10. 贝特立诗黄蜓肾兰

贝特立诗黄蜓肾兰曾在1964年世界胡姬会议上赢得奖项。花枝修长、多枝桠，枝上的花多达六十朵以上。这一配种兰花培育成功至今已有三十年历史，却仍是极受欢迎的剪花枝品种。

Aranthera Beatrice Ng 'Yellow'

10. アランセラ ベアトリス ン "イエロー"

これは、1964年の世界ラン品評会で入賞した交配種です。枝は長く多枝にわかれ、ひとつの枝には60もの黄色い花をつけます。三十年以上も前に作られたものですが、今でも切り花として人気があります。

Ascocenda Peggy Foo

11. *Ascocenda* **Peggy Foo**

A Hawaiian hybrid that is popular with miniature orchid lovers for its densely arranged bright red flowers. Produced in the 1970s it is one of the earliest compact ***Ascocenda*** hybrids.

11. 柏琪符壶唇梵兰

柏琪符壶唇梵兰是夏威夷品种，花朵颜色鲜红、生长稠密，极受爱好袖珍型胡姬者的喜爱。柏琪符壶唇梵兰是七十年代最早的密聚花朵壶唇梵兰配种之一。

11. アスコセンダ　ペギー　フー

これは、ハワイ産の交配品種で、その濃密な深紅の花は。ミニラン愛好家のあいだで人気があります。1970年代に開発された、最も初期の小型アスコセンダの交配品種のひとつです。

12. *Renantanda* Charlie Mason

A hybrid that has won awards in many orchid shows. It is one of the largest and most beautiful of ***Renantanda*** hybrids.

12. 查理马松肾梵兰

查理马松肾梵兰是在胡姬展览会上频频得奖的品种。查理马松肾梵兰是最大和最美的肾梵兰配种之一。

12. レナンタンダ チャーリー メイソン

数々のラン品評会で入賞した交配品種で、レナンタンダ種の中でも最も大きくかつ華麗なもののひとつです。

Renantanda Charlie Mason

Waterfall

13. Waterfall

This is one of two waterfalls in the Gardens. It is made of volcanic rocks and the landscaped display shows off the brilliantly coloured **Renanthera** and **Kagawara**. Also featured here are the invaluable **Cycads**.

13. 瀑布

园里有两处瀑布，这是其中之一。以火山岩筑成，园景设计衬托出肾药兰及贺川氏兰的鲜艳色彩。这里还能见到极其珍贵的苏铁植物。

13. 滝

これは園内にある二つの滝のうちのひとつです。火山岩でつくられていて、全体の風景は、鮮やかな色のレナンセラとカガワラで印象づけられています。また、ここでは、非常に貴重な品種であるサイキャッズ（Cycads）もみることができます。

14. *Vanda* Miss Joaquim

15. *Vanda* Miss Joaquim 'Douglas'

Vanda* Miss Joaquim** is the oldest natural hybrid of Singapore and Malaysia and is the first ***Vanda hybrid to be registered in the world.

It was found in 1893 by Miss Agnes Joaquim, an Armenian lady, in her garden in Tanjong Pagar. This new hybrid was then named after her.

On 15 April 1981, ***Vanda* Miss Joaquim** was made the National Flower of Singapore. It was selected because of its beauty, resilience and year-round blooming quality.

***Vanda* Miss Joaquim 'Douglas'** is the brother of ***Vanda* Miss Joaquim**. It is very similar to ***Vanda* Miss Joaquim** but it is bigger with darker and brighter coloured petals. However, it is not as free flowering.

14. 卓锦万代兰

15. 卓锦万代兰变种"道格拉斯"

卓锦万代兰是生长在新加坡和马来西亚的最早的天然兰花品种，也是全世界最先注册的第一种万代兰品种。

这一品种在1893年由亚美尼亚人爱妮斯卓锦小姐在丹绒百葛的住家花园中发现，因此以她命名。

1981年4月15日，卓锦万代兰被选为新加坡国花。其美丽、坚韧及长年开花的特质，是当选的原因。卓锦万代兰变种"道格拉斯"是卓锦万代兰的"兄弟"，与卓锦万代兰相似，但花朵较大，颜色较深，而且不如卓锦万代兰般长年开花。

▲ *Vanda* Miss Joaquim
▼ *Vanda* Miss Joaquim 'Douglas'

14. バンダ　ミス　ジョーキム

15. バンダ　ミス　ジョーキム
"ダグラス"

バンダ　ミス　ジョーキムは、シンガポールとマレーシアで一番古い自然交配品種で、バンダの交配品種では、世界でも最初に登録されたものです。

名前は、1893年、タンジョンパガーの自宅の庭で最初に発見したアルメニア人、ミス　アグネス　ジョーキムに因んでつけられました。

そして、1981年4月15日、その花の美しさと躍動感、一年中花をつける点から、シンガポールの国花に指定されています。

バンダ　ミス　ジョーキム"ダグラス"は、バンダ　ミス　ジョーキムの兄弟品種で、大変よく似ていますが、形はもっと大きく、弁の色が濃く鮮やかです。開花させやすい品種ではありません。

▲ *Vanda* Miss Joaquim
▼ *Vanda* Miss Joaquim 'Douglas'

16. *Sophrolaeliocattleya* Hawaiian Starlet

This is a popular miniature *Cattleya* which thrives well in Singapore. The bright orange petals and sepals contrast strongly against the red lip, making this hybrid a very showy plant. The plant is hardy and attaches itself easily to a tree.

16. 夏威夷坦乐朱色蕾利卡德丽亚兰

这种受欢迎的袖珍型卡德丽亚兰在新加坡极易生长。花瓣和萼片呈鲜艳的橙色，与红色的花唇形成强烈的对照，使其成为十分抢眼的胡姬配种。夏威夷坦乐朱色蕾利卡德丽亚兰生命力强，容易攀附在树木上生长。

16. ソフィロラエリオカトレア ハワイリアン スターレット

これは、シンガポールでも育てやすい、人気のあるミニ カトレアです。花弁と萼のオレンジ色が、中央部分の赤と、鮮やかな対照をなし、この品種を非常に華やかで極立ったものにみせています。大変丈夫で、木にも簡単に寄生させられます。

Sophrolaeliocattleya Hawaiian Starlet

17. *Mokara* Bibi

This is one of the early *Mokara* hybrids; it was bred for the cut-flower trade about 30 years ago. This hybrid has varieties in colours ranging from light pink to dark red.

17. 比比莫氏兰

比比莫氏兰是早期培育的供应剪花枝市场的莫氏兰配种之一。培育至今约有30年历史。此配种颜色繁多，从淡粉红色至深红色不一。

17. モカラ　ビビ

30年ほど前に、切り花用に栽培された初期のモカラの一種です。淡いピンクから濃い赤まで、その花の色は多様です。

Mokara Bibi

18. *Vanda* Ruby Prince

This hybrid was produced by the Singapore Botanic Gardens. The large dark maroon lip enhances the attractiveness of this orchid.

18. 鲁比太子万代兰

鲁比太子万代兰是新加坡植物园培育的品种。硕大而呈褐红色的特出花唇，增添了鲁比太子万代兰的魅力。

18. バンダ ルビー プリンス

シンガポール熱帯植物の交配品種で、大きくて濃いえび茶色の左右対照の唇形花弁がこのランの魅力です。

Vanda Ruby Prince

19. *Aranda* Majula 'Rimau'

The flowers are fragrant with attractive bars on the sepals and petals. One of the earliest orchids to be used for cut-flowers.

19. 马珠拉"里茂"蜻蜓万代兰

马珠拉"里茂"蜻蜓万代兰花朵含香味，萼片和花瓣上有吸引人的条纹。这是最早作为剪花枝用途的胡姬品种之一。

19. アランダ マジュラ "リマウ"

この花は香りがよく、萼や花弁に美しいしま模様がみられます。ランが切り花に使われ始めた最も初期のもののひとつです。

Aranda Majula 'Rimau'

20. *Mokara* Kelvin 'Orange'

One of the earliest *Mokara* hybrids to be bred locally. This free flowering hybrid produces attractive orange flowers.

20. 卡明橙色莫氏兰

卡明橙色莫氏兰是本地最早培育的莫氏兰配种之一。这长年开花的品种开出迷人的橙色花朵。

20. モカラ ケルビン オレンジ

シンガポールで交配された初期の、モカラ種のひとつで、花も咲かせやすく、鮮明なオレンジ色の花を咲かせます。

Mokara Kelvin 'Orange'

21. *Stamariaara* Noel

This compact hybrid flowers well in full sun. The dark red flower is star shaped with pointed petals and sepals.

21. 惹尔史打马利亚氏兰

惹尔史打马利亚氏兰是一种花朵稠密的配种，在大太阳光照耀下花朵盛开。褐红色的花朵呈星形，花瓣与萼片的边沿呈针状。

21. スタマリアーラ　ノエル

開花のためには充分な陽光が必要な小型種です。深い紅色の花は、星型をしており、とがった花弁と萼をもちます。

Stamariaara Noel

22. *Christieara* Malibu Gold

A medium sized plant with attractive orange-yellow flowers.

22. 马里布金黄克里斯蒂氏兰

马里布金黄克里斯蒂氏兰是一种中型品种，开着引人注目的橙黄色花朵。

Christieara Malibu Gold

22. クリスチェーラ　マリブーゴールド

美しいオレンジイエローの花をつける中型種です。

23. *Vanda* Margaret Tan

This hybrid bears unusually large dark pink blooms. The plant flowers freely under full sun.

23. 马格烈陈万代兰

这配种会开非常罕见的深粉红色的花朵。在大太阳光照耀下花朵盛开。

23. バンダ マーガレット タン

珍しい大きな濃いピンクの花をつけます。充分な陽光さえあれば、簡単に栽培できます。

Vanda Margaret Tan

24. *Dendrobium* Hybrids

Dendrobium is one of largest plant genera in the world. It is also the genus with the most hybrids bred by the Singapore Botanic Gardens. The first Dendrobium hybrid, ***Dendrobium* Helen Park**, was registered in the 1940s. Since then, the Orchid Breeding Programme of the Gardens has produced more than 145 registered hybrids in this genus.

24. 石斛兰杂交品种

石斛兰属是世界兰科植物中的最大属之一，也是植物园中配种最多的单一兰科植物属。在1940年注册的海伦巴石斛兰，是第一个注册的石斛兰品种。从那时开始，在胡姬育种计划下，植物园已培育出超过145种石斛兰属配种，并予注册。

24. デンドロビウム　交配品種

デンドロビウム属は、世界でも最も大きい属のひとつであり、当植物園でも一番多くの交配品種がつくられています。最初の交配品種は、1940年代にデンドロビウム　ヘレン　パークという名で登録されました。以来、当園のラン繁殖計画により、145種をこえる同種の交配品種が登録されています。

Dendrobium Hybrids

▲ *Dendrobium* Seena
▼ *Dendrobium* White Fairy

24a. *Dendrobium* Seena
This plant has flowers that are a soft white with a contrasting purple lip. A popular cut-flower.

24a. 西娜石斛兰
西娜石斛兰花朵呈柔白色，花心带有紫色的点缀，是一种非常受欢迎的剪花枝胡姬。

24a. デンドロビウム　シーナ
中央が紫色がかった、やわらかく白い花です。切り花として人気があります。

24b. *Dendrobium* White Fairy
A white, free flowering orchid widely grown for the cut-flower trade.

24b. 白仙女石斛兰
白仙女石斛兰花朵呈白色，长年开花，是从事剪花枝行业的花农广泛种植的胡姬。

24b. デンドロビウム　ホワイトフェアリー
花は白色で育てやすく、切り花用に栽培されています。

24c. *Dendrobium* Genting Blue
A purplish-blue orchid popular in the cut-flower trade. The plant is free flowering.

24c. 云顶蓝石斛兰
云顶蓝石斛兰是紫蓝色的胡姬，在剪花枝业中极受欢迎。长年开花。

24c. デンドロビウム　ゲンティンブルー
青みがかった紫色の花で、やはり育てやすく、切り花用に多くつくられています。

24d. *Dendrobium* Hiang Beauty
A white ***Dendrobium*** with a beautiful purple centre. The orchid is attractive because of the appealing contrasting colours of the flowers.

24d. 香尔美女石斛兰
香尔美女石斛兰是花朵整体白色并配以紫色唇瓣的石斛兰。强烈的颜色对比，为香尔美女石斛兰带来迷人的魅力。

24d. デンドロビウム　ヒャンビューティー
首の部分が美しい紫色の白いデンドロビウムです。対照的になっている花弁の美しい色彩が目を惹きつけます。

▲ *Dendrobium* Genting Blue
▼ *Dendrobium* Hiang Beauty

Lewisara Fatimah Alsagoff

25. *Lewisara* Fatimah Alsagoff

This is a semi-shade loving epiphytic plant. The flowers are a very attractive violet-blue colour.

25. 法地马阿沙戈夫卢娃沙拉兰

半日阴性的法地马阿沙戈夫卢娃沙拉兰栽植在树干上，花朵呈迷人的紫蓝色。

25. ルーイサラ　ファティマ　アルサゴフ

半日陰性で、木の枝に好んで繁殖する背丈の低いランです。すばらしく魅力的な紫がかった青い花をつけます。

26. *Vanda* Poepoe 'Diana'

This hardy growing plant is closely related to the national flower *Vanda* Miss Joaquim. It usually flowers best in full sun.

26. 泊泊"蒂娜"万代兰

泊泊"蒂娜"万代兰是一种坚强的品种，与国花卓锦万代兰同为一属。在艳阳下，花朵通常开得最为茂盛。

26. バンダ ポーポー "ダイアナ"

丈夫なこのランは国花のバンダ ミス ジョーキムにかなり近い品種です。通常は、充分な陽光のもとで、最も良く花をつけます。

Vanda Poepoe 'Diana'

27. *Aranda* Wong Bee Yeok
This free flowering plant produces one of the largest *Aranda* flowers.

27. 黄美玉蜻蜓万代兰
黄美玉蜻蜓万代兰长年开花，是花朵最大的紫色蜻蜓万代兰品种之一。

27. アランダ　ウオン　ビーイョク
最も大きなアランダ種のひとつで、よく花をつけます。

Aranda Wong Bee Yeok

28. *Dendrobium crumenatum*

A native to Singapore and commonly known as "Pigeon Orchid." The delicate, fragrant flowers open in the morning nine days after a sudden drop in temperature caused for instance by a rain-storm, but will fade by afternoon. This epiphytic orchid is commonly grown on our roadside trees.

上部着生ランは、シンガポールの街路樹の上によくみられます。

Dendrobium crumenatum

28. 鸠斛兰

鸠斛兰是新加坡土产，俗称鸽子兰。通常在温度因骤雨而突然下降后的第九天早上，就会开出有香味的花朵。花朵娇弱不能耐久，当天下午就凋谢。附生类鸽子兰一般长在路边的树上。

28. デンドロビウム クルメナタム

シンガポール原産で、通称、「ピジョン　オーキッド」と呼ばれています。大雨による急激な気温の下降後、九日間程かかって、朝にかぐわしい花を咲かせますが、午後にはしぼんでしまいます。この

29. *Aranda* Christine 'Alba'

This unusual clone of ***Aranda* Christine** produces white flowers with purple spots. The original ***Aranda* Christine** is pink with dark spots.

29. 克丽斯汀"亚巴"蜻蜓万代兰

克丽斯汀"亚巴"蜻蜓万代兰是不常见的品种，花朵呈白色，带蓝色斑点。克丽斯汀蜻蜓万代兰的原本色泽是粉红，带深色斑点。

29. アランダ　クリスティン"アルバ"

アランダ　クリスティンから分離増殖した珍しい花で、紫色の斑点のある白い花を咲かせます。原種のアランダ　クリスティンは、ピンクの地に濃い斑点をもつ花です。

Aranda Christine 'Alba'

30. Tan Hoon Siang Misthouse

In the Tan Hoon Siang misthouse you will see **Cymbidium** hybrids from Holland, **Epidendrum** hybrids from Mexico, **Pansy** orchids from Australia, **Dendrobium nobile** types from Japan, **Antelope dendrobiums** from Papua New Guinea, **Vanda** and **Ascocenda** hybrids from Thailand, **Trichoglottis** and **Renanthera** species from Philippines, and **Dendrobium** hybrids from Singapore.

30. タン　フーン　シアン　ミストハウス

ここでは、世界各国から集められたランの品種を見ることができます。オランダ産シンビヂウムの交配品種、メキシコ産エピデンドラムの交配品種、オーストラリア産のパンジーラン、日本産デンドロビウム　ノービル、パプアニューギニア産アンテロープ　デンドロビウム、タイ産のバンダとアルコセンダの交配品種、フィリピン産のトリコグロチスやレナセラ種、シンガポール産デンドロビウムの交配品種などがあります。

Tan Hoon Siang Misthouse

30. 陈温祥雾室

在国家胡姬园内的陈温祥雾室，可观赏到各种荷兰来的配种惠兰，南美洲墨西哥来的配种树兰，澳洲来的堇色兰，日本来的节生花型石斛兰，新几内亚来的羚角花型石斛兰，泰国来的配种万代兰及壶唇梵兰，菲律宾来的茸舌兰及原种肾药兰，以及新加坡的配种石斛兰。

31. Yuen-Peng McNeice Bromeliad House

To complement the display of orchids, the Yuen Peng McNeice bromeliad collection is featured in the National Orchid Garden. Propagations from this collection of 20,000 air plants representing 800 types in the Pineapple family

31. ユエン　ペン　マクニース　ブロムリアド　ハウス

ランの花々の展示の間に、ユエン　ペン　マクニース　ブロムリアドのコレクションが専用の展示室に展示されています。このコレクションは、パイナップル科を代表する八百種から増殖された二万本もの空中植物から成り、当植物園ならではの特徴の一つとなっています。

Yuen-Peng McNeice Bromeliad House

have also been incorporated in the landscaping of the Garden.

31. 麦婉平夫人凤梨科温室

配合胡姬展，麦婉平夫人凤梨科温室陈列麦婉平夫人所收集的凤梨科品种，展示凤梨科植物的特色。温室所陈列的两万株气根植物，分属八百个凤梨科品种。由此繁殖出来的植物，也移种在园内各处，装点园景。

32. Sundials

There are two sundials in the National Orchid Garden. The first is located in the VIP Orchid Garden and the second in the "winter" zone.

The sundials are set in such a way that the central rod is aligned in a north-south axis. The circular structure reflects that of the Earth's. Both sundials have a belt that represents the equator. The first sundial has lines that represent the longitudes of the earth while the second sundial has lines depicting the Tropics of Cancer and Capricorn.

32. 日晷仪

国家胡姬园有两座日晷仪。第一座设在贵宾胡姬园，第二座设在冬季带。

日晷仪中央的指针是一根南北向的直轴，圆形的结构代表地球。两座日晷仪都有代表赤道的环带。第一座日晷仪有代表地球经度的线条，第二座日晷仪则绘上南北回归线。

32. 日時計

国立ラン園には、日時計が二つあり、ひとつはVIPラン園に、もうひとつは「冬」の庭園にあります。

中心の軸が地軸に平行にセットされていて、循環の仕組みは地球の自転と同時になっています。また、赤道を示す線があり、一方の時計には地球の経度をあらわす線が、もうひとつには南回帰線、北回帰線を示す線があります。

Sundial in VIP Orchid Garden

Orchidarium

33. Orchidarium

This holds our species collection. The Orchidarium is landscaped to simulate the natural orchid habitats of tropical rainforests. There are about 400 species in 97 genera growing in the Orchidarium.

View of Orchidarium

33. 胡姬原种区

这是收集胡姬原种的地区，胡姬原种区仿照胡姬在热带雨林生长的自然环境建成。区内共有97属的400种原种胡姬。

33. オーキダリウム(ラン栽培園)

ここには当園の全品種コレクションが保有されています。熱帯雨林での自然なラン生息地となるように造園されており、現在、約97属400種が栽培されています。

33a. *Dendrobium bigibbum* 'compactum'

Found on the Frangipani at the entrance to the Orchidarium is this miniature species from Australia. Most of our miniature hybrids are derived from this parent.

33a. 碧姬蔓石斛兰

在胡姬原种区进口处的鸡蛋花树上,可以看到碧姬蔓石斛兰。这是从澳洲引进的袖珍型原种石斛兰。目前培育的袖珍型石斛兰配种胡姬,绝大多数出自这袖珍型原种母株。

Dendrobium bigibbum 'compactum'

33a. デンドロビウム　ビギバン

オーストラリア産のミニ品種で、ラン栽培園の入口のフレンジペニの樹木上に見られます。現在ほとんどのミニ交配種は、このランの母株からつくられたものです。

Orchidarium

33b. Terrestrial Orchids

Terrestrial orchids are orchids that grow on the ground. One such orchid on display is ***Spathoglottis plicata***. This species readily produces seed pods.

33b. 地生类胡姬

地生类胡姬就是在地面生长的胡姬。这里展示的地生类胡姬品种，有容易产生朔果的摺叶苞舌兰。

33b. 陸生ラン

陸生ランとは、土のうえに育つ品種のことです。展示されているものは、種がさやに入っているスパトグロチス　プリカータというランです。

Spathoglottis plicata

Orchidarium

33c. Lithophytic Orchids

Lithophytic orchids are those that grow on rocks. On display in the Orchidarium are various varieties of ***Doritis pulcherrima***.

33c. 岩石生类胡姬

岩石生类胡姬就是附生在岩石上的胡姬。这里展示的岩石生类胡姬有各种擎天娥兰。

33c. 岩石生ラン

岩石生ランとは、岩や石の上に育つランのことです。ここでは、ドリティス プルチェリマの多様な品種が展示されています。

Doritis pulcherrima

Orchidarium

33d. Epiphytic Orchids

These are orchids that grow on trunks and branches of trees. An interesting feature is the tremendous diversity of leaf-forms. The flowers are often small.

33d. 附生类胡姬

这里展示的是长在树干和树枝的附生类胡姬。附生类胡姬极端多样化的叶形是其有趣的特色。花朵普遍极小。

33d. 上部着生ラン

木の幹や枝の上で育つランです。花は大変小さいものでむしろ、非常に特徴のある形をした葉のほうに注目してください。

Epiphytic Orchids

Orchidarium

33e. Slipper Orchids

Paphiopedilums are found next to the trellis in the orchidarium. They are called Slipper orchids because of the shape of their lips. They are either terrestrial or lithophytic.

33e. 拖鞋兰

在胡姬原种区格子棚的旁边,可以看到拖鞋兰。因其唇瓣状似拖鞋,故名。拖鞋兰属于地生类或岩石生类胡姬。

33e. スリッパーラン

パフィオペディラムは、ラン栽培園の格子垣のとなりにあり、その花の中央部の形から、スリッパー ランと呼ばれています。陸生型かあるいは岩石生型のどちらかです。

A Slipper Orchid

Orchidarium

View of Orchidarium Waterfall

33f. Orchidarium Waterfall
The waterfall in the orchidarium helps to create the humid micro-climate that these orchids need. Those planted here include ***Grammatophyllum speciosum***, ***Epidendrum radicans***, ***Doritis pulcherrima***, ***Spathoglottis affinis*** and ***Phalaenopsis violacea***.

33f. 胡姬原种区瀑布
胡姬原种区的瀑布，在区内创造一个潮湿的微气候，提供胡姬所需要的生长环境。在瀑布旁生长的胡姬，有：巨兰、树兰、天蛾兰、苞舌兰和蝴蝶兰。

33f. ラン栽培室の滝
この滝は、湿気のある気候を必要とするランのためにつくられています。ここでは、グラマトフィラム　スペシオスム、エピデンドラム、ラディカンズ、ドリティス　プルチェリマ、スパソグロティス、アフィニィス、ファラノプシィス、ビィオラセアなどが見られます。

33g. *Arundina graminifolia*
This orchid is widespread in Southeast Asia. It is also known as "bamboo orchid" because of its bamboo-like habit. The flowers have large lips and superficially they look like a *Cattleya*.

33g. 穗叶竹兰
穗叶竹兰在东南亚一带分布很广。它具有细长的竹叶形叶子,因而得名。花朵唇瓣大,外形与卡德丽亚兰相似。

33g. アランヂナグラミニフォリア
東南アジアでも広域で見られる種類です。細竹に似た葉の形からバンブー オーキッドとも呼ばれています。その花は、大きな中央突出部分をもち、外観上はカトレアに類似しています。

Arundina graminifolia

Orchidarium

33h. Rat Tail Orchids
Species of **Paraphalaenopsis** are so named because their long cyclindrical leaves resemble the form of rats' tails.

33h. 鼠尾兰
拟蝴蝶兰原种，俗称鼠尾兰，长圆筒状的叶形像老鼠尾巴，因而得名。

33h. ねずみのしっぽラン
パラファリエノプシス種であるこのランはその長い円筒形の葉がねずみのしっぽに似ているところから、この名前がつきました。

A Rat Tail Orchid

Orchidarium

33i. *Epidendrum cinnabarinum*
Commonly known as "reed orchid." This orchid was introduced into Singapore from South America. A sun-loving orchid that is easy to grow and is free-flowering.

33i. 树兰
树兰俗称草胡姬,是由南美洲引进新加坡的品种。这类胡姬喜爱阳光,容易生长,长年开花。

33i. エピデンドラムシンナバリナム
一般には、リード(葦)オーキッドという名で知られ、南米からやってきました。日光を好み、育てやすく花も咲かせやすいランです。

Epidendrum cinnabarinum

34. VIP Orchid Garden

The orchid breeding programme of the Singapore Botanic Gardens was initiated by Prof. Eric Holttum in 1928. The outstanding hybrids from this programme established the reputation of the Gardens' orchid programme.

To date, the Gardens has named over 90 VIP orchids. The first VIP orchid was ***Aranthera* Anne Black** in 1956, after Lady Black, wife of a former Governor of Singapore, Sir Robert Black. Other VIP orchids on display include ***Dendrobium* Margaret Thatcher**, ***Renantanda* Akihito**, ***Dendrobium* Masako Kotaishi Hidenka**, ***Dendrobium* Asean Beauty**, ***Dendrobium* Memoria Princess Diana** and ***Vandaenopsis* Nelson Mandela**.

View of VIP Orchid Garden

As Singapore orchids gained fame, it became obvious that they should be used as agents to promote goodwill and closer ties between nations. From 1957 the Singapore Government began to honour State Visitors and other VIPs by naming selected orchid hybrids after them. This prized collection of "VIP Orchids" has become an important attraction of the National Orchid Garden.

VIP Orchid Garden

34. 贵宾胡姬园

1928年，艾力克霍尔特姆教授在新加坡植物园率先进行胡姬育种研究。在他精心研究下，成功培植出了各种不同胡姬花的配种，奠定了植物园胡姬育种的声誉。

新加坡胡姬扬名国际后，很自然地成为促进国与国之间的亲善与紧密关系的媒介。1957年以来，新加坡政府就开始以国宾和本外地要人的姓名，为特选的胡姬配种命名，以此表示敬意。这些以贵宾命名的珍贵胡姬，收集在贵宾胡姬园内，已经成为国家胡姬园一个吸引游人的重点。

至今，国家胡姬园已经有超过九十种以贵宾命名的胡姬。第一种以贵宾命名的胡姬，是1956年以前新加坡总督罗拔布拉克爵士的夫人安妮布拉克命名的安妮布拉克蜓肾兰。贵宾胡姬园展示的其他贵宾胡姬，包括以前英国首相玛格烈撒切尔夫人命名的石斛兰，以前日本明仁太子命名的肾药兰，日本皇太子妃雅子命名的石斛兰，亚细安美女石斛兰纪念戴安娜太子妃石斛兰以及尼森曼德拉蝴蝶梵兰。

34. VIP ラン園

シンガポール熱帯植物園でのラン繁殖計画は、1928年、エリックホルタム教授の手で始められました。この計画から生まれたすばらしい混成種は、当植物園のラン・プログラムの評価をゆるぎないものにしています。

シンガポールのランは、好評を博するにつれて、国際親善の役割を果たすようにもなりました。1957年以来、シンガポール政府は、国の内外からの国賓、公賓やVIPに

View of VIP Orchid Garden

敬意を表して、選ばれたランの混成種に彼らの名前を称しています。このVIPランのすばらしいコレクションは、わが熱帯植物園の重要な魅力でもあります。

現在までに、90をこえるVIPランに名前がつけられていますが、最初のVIPランは1956年に、元シンガポール統治者、サー ロバート ブラックの妻、レディ ブラックからつけられた アランセラ アン ブラックです。また、デンドロビウム マーガレット サッチャー、レナンタンダ アキヒト、デンドロビウム プリンセス マサコ、デンドロビウム エィシャン

VIP Orchid Garden

ビューティー、デンドロビウム　メモリア　プリンセス　ダイアナ　そしてバンダノプシス　ネルソン　マンデラなども展示されています。

Dendrobium Memoria Princess Diana

Dendrobium Asean Beauty

Vandaenopsis Nelson Mandela

Dendrobium Masako Kotaishi Hidenka

35. Burkill Hall

Constructed in 1866, Burkill Hall is the focal point of the National Orchid Garden. It was once home to the Gardens' directors. The house commands a spectacular view of the orchid garden and the surrounding terrain including Palm Valley and the rainforest beyond. Two generations of Burkills have resided in this colonial bungalow. Issac Henry Burkill was the Gardens' director from 1912-25. His son, Humphrey Morrison Burkill, was born in this house. He was the last director (1957-69) to live in Burkill Hall. He saw the Gardens through the crucial transition from British leadership to local leaders.

Burkill Hall has been named as one of Singapore's monuments of architectural and historical interest by the Preservation of Monuments Board. It has been renovated and conserved to be used as a VIP Reception and Events Hall.

35. 伯克厅

伯克厅在1866年建成，是国家胡姬园的主要建筑。伯克厅曾经是新加坡植物园几位总管的居所。这建筑物俯瞰胡姬园及周围地域，包括棕榈谷及另一边的雨林。

伯克两代人在此英国式的别墅居

住过。伊萨亨利伯克于1912-25年间出任植物园总管。他的儿子汉福利摩里申伯克在这别墅出世，是最后一位居住在伯克厅的植物园总管 (1957-69年)。他见证了植物园管辖权从英国政府移交给新加坡政府的重要历史时刻。

伯克厅已被国家历史建筑物保留局列为具有建筑学与历史意义的保留建筑物之一。伯克厅经过全面装修，保留作为款待贵宾和举行重要活动之用。

Burkill Hall

35. バーキル　ホール

1866年に建てられたバーキル ホールは、国立ラン園の中心に位置し、以前は、植物園長の住宅でした。この建て物からは、ラン園のすばらしい眺望をはじめ、椰子の谷や熱帯雨林をふくむ周囲の地形が一望のもとに望めます。

バーキル家の二世代にわたる家族がこのコロニアル風の家に住んでいました。アイザック　ヘンリー　バーキルは、1912年から1925年まで園長でした。息子のハンフリー　モリソン　バーキルは、この家で生まれ、バーキル ホールに住んで最後の園長として、1957年から1969年まで務めました。彼は、植物園がイギリス人主導からシンガポール人の手へと渡る厳しい過渡期の時代を見守ったことになります。

バーキル ホールは、記念物保存局によって、シンガポールの建築史と歴史的記念物のひとつとして指定され、現在は、VIPの接待所やイベントホールとして利用する目的で、復元、保存されています。

INDEX OF ORCHIDS　ランの目録　胡姫索引

	Page		Page
Antelope dendrobiums	49	*Epidendrum radicans*	58
Arachnis Maggie Oei	23	*Grammatophyllum speciosum*	22
Aranda Christine 'Alba'	48	*Lewisara* Fatimah Alsagoff	44
Aranda Majula 'Rimau'	36	*Mokara* Bibi	34
Aranda Wong Bee Yeok	46	*Mokara* Chark Kuan	26
Aranthera Anne Black	62	*Mokara* Kelvin 'Yellow'	20
Aranthera Batrice Ng 'Yellow'	27	*Mokara* Kelvin 'Orange'	37
Arudina graminifolia	59	*Mokara* Sayan	25
Ascocenda hybrids	49	*Mokara* Zaleha Alsagoff	24
Ascocenda Peggy Foo	28	*Oncidium* Goldiana 'Golden Shower'	19
Christiaara Malibu Gold	39		
Cymbidium hybrids	49	*Paraphalaenopsis* species	60
Dendrobium Asean Beauty	64	*Phalaenopsis violacea*	58
Dendrobium bigibbum 'compactum'	53	*Renantanda* Akihito	8, 62
		Rats' Tail orchids	60
Dendrobium Chanel	21	*Renantanda* Charlie Mason	29
Dendrobium crumenatum	47	*Renantanda* Prince Norodom Sihanouk	8
Dendrobium hybrids	41		
Dendrobium Genting Blue	43	*Renanthera* species	49
Dendrobium Helen Park	41	Slipper orchids	57
Dendrobium Hiang Beauty	43	*Spathoglottis affinis*	58
Dendrobium Margaret Thatcher	8, 62	*Spathoglottis plicata*	54
		Sophrolaeliocattleya Hawaiian Starlet	33
Dendrobium Memoria Princess Diana	8, 62		
		Stamariaara Noel	38
Dendrobium nobile	49	*Trichoglottis* species	49
Dendrobium Princess Masako	62	*Vanda* hybrids	49
Dendrobium Seena	42	*Vanda* Margaret Tan	40
Dendrobium Singapore Girl Orchid	6	*Vanda* Miss Joaquim	31
		Vanda Miss Joaquim 'Douglas'	31
Dendrobium White Fairy	42	*Vanda* Poepoe 'Diana'	45
Doritis pulcherrima	55	*Vanda* Ruby Prince	35
Epidendrum cinnabarinum	61	*Vandaenopsis* Nelson Mandela	8, 64
Epidendrum hybrids	49		

67

Acknowledgements

We warmly thank Chin See Chung for his patience in editing the manuscript, Yam Tim Wing for his technical assistance and for reading the manuscript, Abdul Hamid Bin Hassan, Yap Siow Hong and Koh Wei Kee for proof reading and other logistical assistance, and Yusof Alsagoff, Peter Ang and our colleagues from the Singapore Botanic Gardens for sharing their slides.

Translation

We express our warmest appreciation to the translators, without whom the Chinese and Japanese versions would not have been possible:

Lim-Ho Chee Len and
Koh-Low Neok Chein for the Chinese translation; and

Staff of the Japanese Supplementary School, Singapore for the Japanese Translation.